The Decoding of the Mystery of

Rennes le Chateau

The Da Vinci Code

Andrew G Frew

Dedicated

To

Henry Lincoln

Note from Author

Rennes-le-Château

The Rennes-le-Château mystery and too the man that brought this obscure mystery to the public attention, Henry Lincoln this book is dedicated and forms the first part of this work. It is the story of a terrible secret found in coded parchments discovered by Bérenger Saunière a local priest who left clues of its location.

What was the secret that Saunière knew? Why did he have written *Terribilis est locus iste* above his Church door? Was there some terrible secret inside? Why did he desecrate the grave of Marie de Nègre d'Ables? Did he realize she knew this secret and had it coded on her gravestone? Was this secret harmful to the Catholic Church? Can this terrible secret be that the body of the KING is in fact Jesus and he was buried there?

Through deciphering of these codes we shall make our journey through France to a Roc to discover the secret of the Templar's.

The Da Vinci Code

Scholars, researchers and experts alike all agree there is no such thing as a Da Vinci Code. In this work we shall reexamine the case and reveal my findings not the one sensationalized but one found in geometry revealing Leonardo's belief in the illuminati, discovery of which, will cast a new understanding upon his art.

Andrew G Frew

London

PART ONE
Rennes-le-Château

PART TWO
The Da Vinci Code

APPENDIX
Photographs
The Gospel of Mary Magdalene

PART ONE

Rennes-le-Château

PART ONE

In part two we are going to examine if there is a Da Vinci code a mystery just as mysterious as this one located on a hill top overlooking the beautifully pretty green landscape of medieval France, the village of Rennes-le-Château. I remember holding in my hand a book Treasure Island by Robert Louis Stevenson, what intrigued me was the first turn of the page a treasure map.

This story is no less intriguing but with one difference it is not a fictional story there is lost secret treasure but nobody as yet has found it. Except maybe one, a priest named Bérenger Saunière who will figure quite a lot in this story. But first our story begins in an old dusty book shop five decades ago when Henry Lincoln picked up a paperback that contained the intriguing story of a penniless priest who it was said after having found old treasure went from being rags to super riches. The interest in this oddity would've stopped there but for the deciphering skills of Lincoln.

The author of this book provided a parchment (Fig a) that was left as a clue and the author did not mention any coded message but the hidden code was discovered by Henry Lincoln in 1969. He found a number of letters to be raised above the rest on the parchment, and simply reading these in order gave him words:

THIS TREASURE BELONGS TO DDGOBERT II

KING AND TO SION AND HE IS THERE DEAD

So began the quest of Henry Lincoln who went on to do three BBC documentaries surrounding the decoding of this mystery. Now we shall take a look at the mystery of Rennes-le-Château.

(Fig a) The text on this parchment is a composite of different Gospel accounts of *Jesus* and his disciples eating corn on the Sabbath.

Our story begins when Bérenger Saunière priest to the diocese of Rennes-le-Château undertook renovations of his Church he found some old parchments within the altar stone. He sent the workmen home for the day and spent the night deciphering the parchments. The next day he told the workmen to lift a stone in front of the altar. When the stone was raised it revealed a crypt, having gone down inside it Saunière then reappeared with a plate containing trinkets, which on questioning from the workmen, he said, it was nothing. Saunière gave the workmen the rest of the day off and they immediately ran to their village and told the story of the find. This stone in front of the altar is interesting for the reverse side shows two knights riding on a horse the same as the symbol for the Seal for Knights Templar. A Catholic military order recognised in 1139 by the papal bull *Omne datum optimum.* These men were like the British SAS or the American SEALS of their day a tough warrior class of monk who protected pilgrims visiting the Holy Land against robbery.

The knights stone from Mary Magdalene Church

Seal for Knights Templar

Around the years 1118 or 1119 a group of nine Knights from the Champagne region of France and all interconnected by family bloodline grouped together to form a guard to protect pilgrims on route to the Holy Lands. These Knights established a base camp in Jerusalem on the south eastern platform of the Holy Temple Mount which stands on Solomon's Temple. Historians believe their real motive was not to protect travelling pilgrims but to treasure hunt for any priceless holy relics beneath the Temple Mount. Many deep tunnels have been found under the Temple Mount created by these knights showing evidence of their excavations. What did they find? If anything, was it the hidden treasures of Solomon buried under the Mount during the Jewish revolt against the Romans in 66 A.D. It is possible these Knights had access to the copper scroll that contained all the locations of the hidden treasures amounting to 200 tons of gold. What we do know is that they were not there that long for in 1128 they were back in Europe. Did they find and bring with them the treasures of Solomon, The Ark of the Covenant? The Holy Grail maybe lost manuscripts we will never know for sure they were a secret organization. Soon after they became a very rich and powerful organization and more Knights joined them. They ruled and administered for 200 years in Western Europe.

Rumors of unholy behavior about them were being circulated finally reaching the Pope, it was said they worshipped a goats head, they had strange rituals and so gradually they fell out of favor with Christendom. On Friday 13th 1307 King Philip IV of France with blessings of the Pope ordered de Molay the grand master and scores of Templar's to be simultaneously arrested. It appears the main motive of the King was to get his hands on the Templar treasures but though searched for high and low was never found it had all been hidden away by the Templar's.

The Templar's are important to solving the Rennes-le-Château mystery. Saunière found something but more importantly was led to his treasures by deciphering the old cryptic parchments. The parchments were placed there by his predecessor, Abbé Antoine Bigou, who had recovered it from an earlier hiding place on the deathbed instructions of Marie de Nègre d'Ables.

Henry Lincoln one time actor, documentary broadcaster and co author of the *Holy Blood and the Holy Grail* (1982) was the first to decipher the parchment and below is what he decoded.

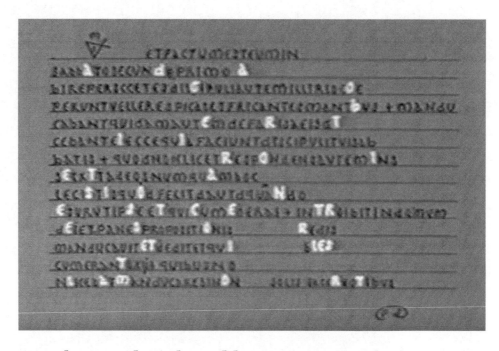

First parchment deciphered by Henry Lincoln he noticed the raised letters spelt a message

Translated

THIS TREASURE BELONGS TO DDGOBERT II

KING AND TO SION AND HE IS THERE DEAD

Who was King DDGOBERT II? Apparently this is a reference to Dagobert II who was a Merovingian King of the Franks that ruled Austrasia, the middle Rhine area of the Franks between 676 until his death in 679. On the death of his father Sigebert III he was prevented from the succession and sought sanctuary in Ireland as a monk in the monastery of Slane. After his cousin was assassinated he regained the throne. Narrative history says he was a bit of a tyrant he made wars, was against the Church and imposed new taxes. He also introduced a new gold coinage.

The Visigoth pillar said to be where the parchments were found.

Within this Visigoth pillar that stands outside the Church it is claimed Bérenger Saunière found the old parchments. It was placed in the garden with a statue of Mary placed on top and inscribed at the bottom with the inscription MISSION 1891.

This pillar is a replica made of resin the original now stands in the museum to prevent vandalism from crazy treasure hunters. Apparently according to the workmen Saunière actually found three things, a collection of old coins, a bracelet and necklace of Visigoth origin and a old chalice not such an insignificant find.

Are these the coins Saunière found the coinage of Dagobert II?

Returning to the message it states this treasure belongs to Sion the name for Jerusalem and what are we to make of the phrase 'AND HE IS THERE DEAD.' Who, is there dead, Dagobert II?

We need to do a little more research surrounding this story to assimilate its origins. As the reader can see this is very much a French mystery and any modern day code breaker should be endowed with that language with a flair for Greek and Latin. The origin of the Rennes-le-Château mystery begins with Marie de Nègre d'Ables it was her grave Saunière desecrated after his return from Paris no doubt to hide clues that unlock this puzzle.

Chateau Hautpoul

Marie de Nègre d'Ables was born in 1714 her ancestors were bailiffs for the kings of the Pay de Sault, a valley not far from Rennes-le-Château. In 1732 she married Francois d'Hautpoul Rennes and through him had four children. Three girls and a boy who later died in infancy, so the male bloodline died out. Her husband Francois died in 1732 he was the last Seigneur de Rennes in the male line. Marie spent the next 28 years living at the manor house Chateau Hautpoul with Marie Anne-Elizabeth d'Hautpoul who was one of her three daughters. She appears to have had financial worries for she sold parts of her inheritance throughout her life. Marie de Nègre d'Ables died on the 17th January 1781 and was buried in the cemetery plot for noble women at Mary Magdalene Church, Rennes-le-Château. The priest at the time was Antoine Bigou who was a family friend and confidant, who helped out on business matters. Before she died apparently on her deathbed she unveiled to Bigou, a family secret of the Hautpoul's and, he in turn left clues to what and where that secret could be found. Hence the importance of her gravestone in deciphering the mystery for one side reveals what that secret was while the other side of it, where that secret lies.

Gravestone of Marie de Nègre d'Ables

Bérenger Saunière

Catholic priest of Rennes-le-Château from 1885 -1917

On discovery of the parchments he went to Paris to get them decoded. He paid a visit to the Louvre and purchased copies of paintings by Pousin and Tennier. On his return he soon began his building projects at **Rennes-le-Château** and money was no object. After 20 years he had spent 1,500 000 million francs.

Saunière was an intelligent and educated man the messages on the parchment code like Henry Lincoln he found by himself, but what made Saunière deface the inscription on the gravestone of

Marie de Nègre d'Ables she that had provided the parchments. Was there another secret message hidden on the tombstone? Fortunately a tomb inscriber had noted the grave markings and published them in a book, leaving the transcription to posterity.

So I have come to a very rapid conclusion if Saunière wanted to cover up the clues why did he not destroy the two parchments. Unless he felt for the time being he could keep them safe. But as for the gravestone it would be open to decipherment of others.

The skeptic would ask. Did he really find parchments? Did he really go to Paris with them? Did he purchase there paintings, is there evidence of this? In any case why would he need to go to Paris, copies of paintings are found in an art book? Some would suggest if he already decoded one for he discovered the trinkets in the crypt, why seek the need in professional help in decoding.

Because the first parchment is very easy to decipher the answer just leaps out of the page the second is very strongly coded quite indecipherable unless one has the key. A lot of work went into this cipher. When apparently it was later decoded the message appeared just meaningless a lot of effort for absolutely nothing.

Therefore I am not so interested in decoding these parchments than I am in deciphering the tombstone much more interesting. I am going to attempt to decode the face side of the headstone fortunately a lot of the ground work has been done by Henry Lincoln who noticed incorrect spellings in the French. It cannot be stressed more the correct deciphering of this stone will give the clue key words to solving the mystery of Rennes-le-Château. Though with the greatest respect, I beg to differ from Lincoln's decipherment of the inscription as MORT epee or Death sword. His mistake was he overlooked using a Pentacle as the key code.

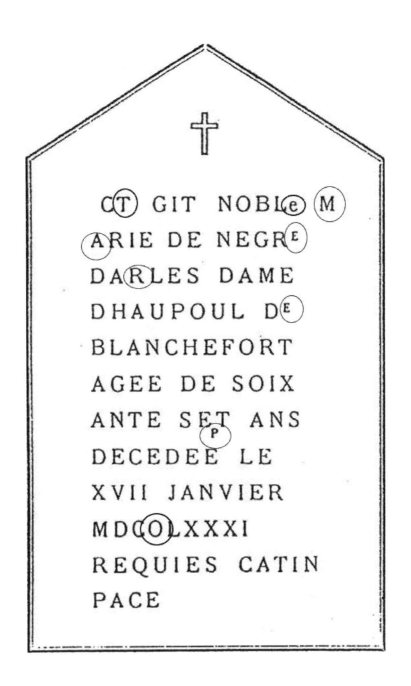

There are nine deliberate mistakes on the stone.

By taking these mistakes as co ordinates the shape of a Pentacle is formed whose point at the crucifix adds the letter (L). Now the key words are decipherable and help us unfold this mystery. This is the first time the stone has been decoded in this manner and reveals an extraordinary discovery the origin of our secret.

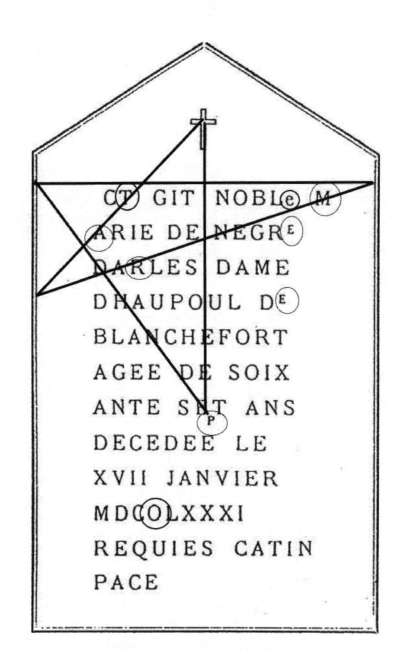

The stone reads TeMpLAR O   EE

TEMPLAR ORDER RENNES

Order of Solomon's Temple, the **Knights Templar**
a Catholic military order recognised in 1139 by the papal
bull *Omne datum optimum*. This indicates the treasure of
Rennes-le-Château is the lost treasure of the TEMPLARS.

There have been suspicions from the very beginning linking the mystery of Rennes-le-Château around the history of the Knights Templar. Legends in the area abound around them because of the suspicions that they hid part of their treasures in the region. Many treasures like the Holy Grail, the Ark of the Covenant and even the myth of Jesus Christ being buried there. It is a fact that three members of the Knights Templar did reside at Rennes-le-Château Lord of Bezu and two brothers from the Reddas family.

The face side of Marie de Nègre d'Ables gravestone suggests her of Templar Order Rennes, Francois d'Hautpoul Rennes, whose bloodline had died out, and with it the secret of the Templar's. Marie de Nègre d'Ables was disclosing a family hidden secret and Bérenger Saunière realised its significance. The Templar's secret he must of thought was its lost treasure artifacts from the Temple Mount acquired by the Templar's but subsequently lost.

This realization gave him impetus too his endeavors he took a trip to Paris no doubt to seek help in decoding the manuscript but more than likely to gain contact with the elite of Parisian society. His first move was to introduce himself to Emma Calve the famous opera singer who no doubt had many of the kinds of acquaintances he sort. His purpose was to extract support from her wealthy friends through monetary beneficiaries they in turn would gain from his finds of lost treasure at Rennes-le-Château.

On his return from Paris he started to exhibit very odd behavior he was caught by the locals rummaging around the cemetery in the dead of night desecrating the graves. One such grave was Dame Marie de NEGRE D'ABLES, he chiseled away the stone markings, but fortunately we still have an accurate copy of that inscription. It was soon after this gallivanting about he gained limitless resources. He built a water tower on the hill to supply the villagers. He constructed the magnificent La Tour Magdala containing his library. After he built a grand Château he began entertaining the very famous members of Paris' elite society like Claude Debussy and Emma Calve who it is said he had an affair.

Emma Calve who it is said had an affair with Saunière

He went on to entertain the French minister of culture and also the cousin to the emperor of Austria. The Vatican meanwhile wondered about the source of this new found wealth. He spared no extravagance with his renovations he had the 'stations of the cross,' installed, a new altar, more statues and a fresco of the Sermon on the Mount and installed new gardens. In total he spent one and half million francs in his renovations. Before this exuberance his total expenditure was about six francs a month!

Fresco of the Sermon on the Mount showing a money bag

The bursting money bag is positioned over the French words

'VOUS TOUS QUI SOUFFLER ET QUI ETES ACCALES'

'You all who blow up, all who weighed down'

La Tour Magdala

Surrounded by a library, a log fire, quietness, I could see myself enjoying the pleasant evenings here in creative solitude. Before Saunière died he was making plans to spend a further 8, 000 000 million francs so who knows what is still to be discovered. The natural thought would be there still treasure in the crypt. I would gather it has been thoroughly searched since his death. Where could be hidden relics to the value of what he intended to spend. It appears he left clues to his fortune in his Church we see this in subtle hints in every statue and fresco. His maid and confident Marie Denarnaud gave indications that she also knew his secret and was going to pass it on but illness prevented her.

St ROCH

St Roch was the patron Saint of plagues. The raised garment of
the knee suggests Freemason initiation. The meaning for each
statue will become abundantly clear as we progress our search.

Mary Magdalene Church

One last clue when Saunière had renovated his Church he had 'stations of the cross,' painted on the walls. One such 'station' in particular stands out. A black boy holds a dish for Pilate to wash his hands while in the background it could be Saunière himself, blessing a location while before him Jesus is lead to his death.

Just to recount again the story so far, during renovation work on the Church Saunière finds old parchments underneath one of the altar pillars the Visigoth pillar that now stands outside the Church. Another story is he found them in a glass vile that rolled out of one of the wooden pillars before being flung on the fire. We still don't know for sure how he found them but we are certain they were placed there by his predecessor, Abbé Antoine Bigou on behalf of Dame Marie de Nègre d'Ables a noble lady of the region. The parchments themselves contain gospel passages and to the undiscerning eye they would mean nothing, but the fact they were purposefully hidden on the authority of the Abbé lies there importance. It did not take Saunière long to realize these parchments must contain a coded message. He must've spent the night decoding and then tested the validity of the hidden code by getting his workmen to lift up the heavy knights stone in front of the altar. Beneath this stone lay the entrance to the Church crypt, he went down its steps that lead down into a small area and there found ancient coins, a jeweled necklace and bracelet and a chalice, the cipher was true. He must've spent many nights after trying to decipher other parchments but being unable he made plans to go to Paris to seek help in its decipherment. Apparently we know it was finally decoded for he sought out the paintings of Poussin and Teniers the master painters whose names are hidden within the parchment cipher.

The reader should be aware the story I have just related is the official one, there is in truth nothing certain in this mystery. It's also possible these events never occurred. That the parchments we have could be a fake actually written by Saunière himself. The first parchment is in school boy code and in truth tells us nothing at all. The second parchment is so difficult to decipher you would need a Bletchley park team to crack it. When it was decoded once again it told us nothing that we already knew. I will explain this later. So the parchments we have could be a fake. If there were any original parchments they were probably destroyed long ago by Saunière himself because he defaced the grave inscription of Dame Marie de Nègre d'Ables he went out of his way to removing the message and it follows he would of destroyed the original parchments also. Lincoln found the shape of a Pentacle within the first parchment but in truth you could if you wished create any shape from among the letters. The second parchment once decoded can be interpreted as gibberish and relating to the Church of Mary Magdalene.

We know that the grave inscription of Dame Marie de Nègre d'Ables was published by an inscriber of gravestones we also know that Saunière was unaware of that fact or he would not have bothered to deface it. So in solving this mystery it should begin here. The search for a key word and the location of the secret would here be unfolded through the correct deciphering of the stone. The parchments if there were any could never have been found in the Visigoth pillar, because the pillar is made of solid stone and has no cavity to support parchments. So we are left with only two facts known for sure in this mystery. The true rendition of the inscription engraved on the tombstone of Marie de Nègre d'Ables and the fact that Bérenger Saunière a poor Catholic priest in the Diocese of Rennes-le-Château, Rennes became rich overnight to the consternation of the Vatican.

We start at the beginning of this treasure hunt, if indeed this is what it is, from Mary Magdalene Church then our journey will take us across the beautiful valleys of Rennes in search of what appears to be the lost treasure of the Templar's. I am going to attempt to decode the back face of the headstone of Marie de Nègre d'Ables fortunately once again a lot of the ground work has been done by Lincoln, though my conclusions are different.

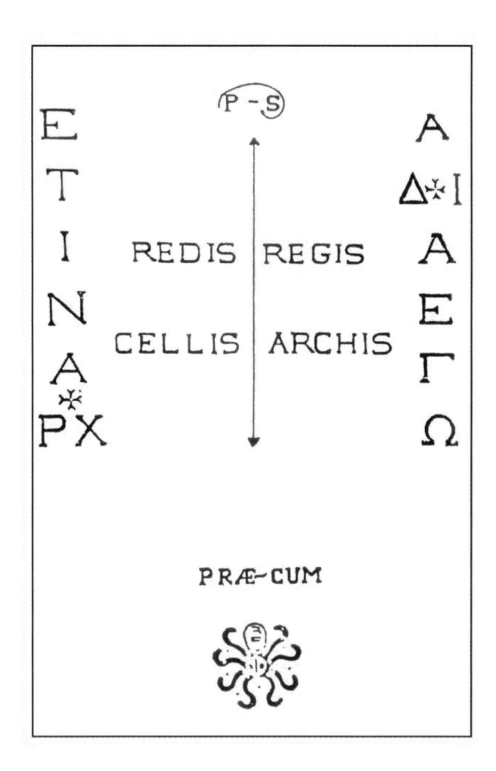

The inscriptions on the tombstone of Dame Marie de NEGRE D'ABLES, d. 17 January 1781 is found the cipher P-S the same inscription on the first parchment. An arrowed line from P-S runs straight down the page pointing to an 8 legged spider.

 **Is connected to**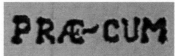

PRAE means 'before,' CUM means, 'with.' Taking the letters before P-S in the alphabet we get O-R

Now we must combine the O-R 'with' ©

We get ORC or ROC

In the French language *(= substance)* roche *f*
(hard, solid) roc *m*

Or ROCK (English)

The line down the center of the page running through REDIS REGIS CELLIS ARCHIS points to the ROC with

 A spider or ARAIGNEE (French) giving ARENNE thus we have:

ROC RENNES

Now we are faced with an enigma, what rock in Rennes? What is found at the rock? The answer lies in the translation of the inscription in the center of the stone.

REDIS REGIS CELLIS ARCHIS

REPEAT KING BODY DEAD

Therefore we have

REPEAT KING BODY DEAD, ROC RENNES

If we recall the deciphering of the first parchment we got

THIS TREASURE BELONGS TO DDGOBERT II

KING AND TO SION AND HE IS THERE DEAD

Who is there dead?

If the dead body is that of DDGOBERT II why would Marie de Nègre d'Ables go to the trouble to put that information again on her gravestone? In fact was KING BODY DEAD, ROC RENNES someone more important telling us the location of Jesus Christ. Is it possible the dead body of Christ was carried to France by

Mary Magdalene and that secret was known by the Templar's? There are legends of her arrival with Mary the mother of Jesus.

The fourteenth station of the cross

Much thought has gone into this apparently innocent retelling of the placing of Jesus in the tomb. But is it, for Jesus is being moved at night as we see the dark night sky and the full moon. One questions whether he being put in the tomb or is taken out.

In Jewish law, a dead body could not be left exposed overnight. The historian Josephus described how the Jews regarded this law as so important that even the bodies of crucified criminals would be taken down and buried before sunset.

The lettering at the sides of the gravestone inscription is easier to decipher because it is in Latin. This gives us important information in finding the location of ROC RENNES.

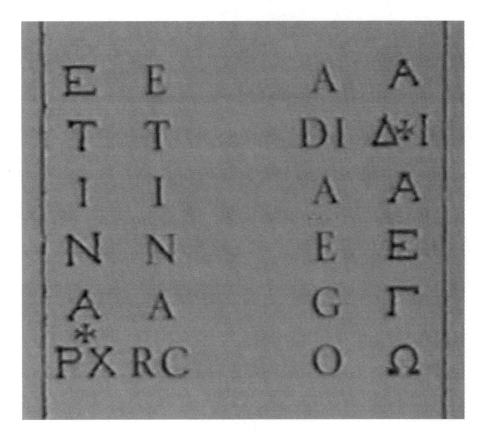

When the Latin on the tombstone is translated it reads;

ET IN ARCADIA EGO

This is the inscription found on the tomb of the painting by Nicolas Poussin 1638. The translation of the phrase is "Even in Arcadia, there am I". So for more clues we must look at this painting.

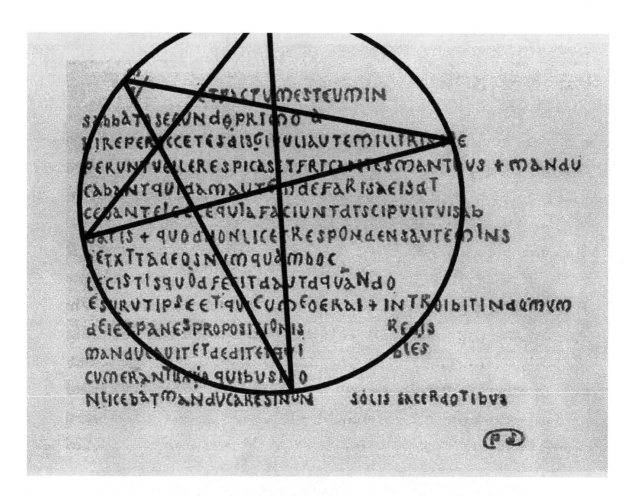

The decoded first parchment

Before I proceed I want to deal with the decipherment of the two parchments the work of Lincoln who studied it for decades.

Basing the start point of the pentacle on the triangle set at the top of the parchment Henry Lincoln made an inspirational discovery he found the Pentacle shape hidden within the message. Unfortunately nobody as yet has deciphered its meaning. There can be no doubt that this is a major clue that unlocks this mystery to finding the location of the secret.

Note the inscription P-S at the bottom A KEY to the mystery. Its importance cannot be underestimated for the same figure was found on a grave stone in the Church Mary Magdalene.

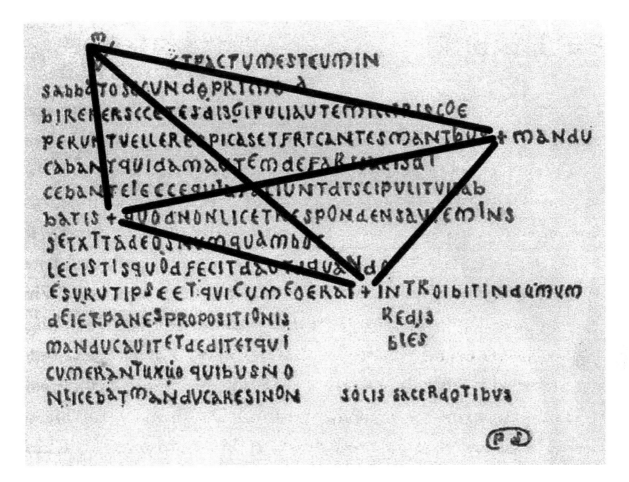

First parchment

The above is my attempt at finding some recognizable shape using the three crosses in the parchment and surprisingly I made a paper letter meaning message.

S

I

O

N

SION =Jerusalem

The second parchment like the first contains Gospel passages.

After much code cracking the parchment was decoded.

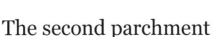

The second parchment

The above is my attempt at finding some recognizable shape using the 2d, d2, b2 code. It forms a Pyramid and is symbolic of the mountain of light, white rock.

"Did ye never read in the Scriptures, The stone which the builders rejected, the same is become the head of the corner: this is the Lord's doing, and it is marvelous in our eyes?"

(Matt. 21:42).

SHEPHERDESS NO TEMPTATION
TO WHICH POUSSIN TENIERS HOLD
THE KEY PEACE 681 BY THE
CROSS AND THIS HORSE OF GOD
I COMPLETE THIS DAEMON GUARDIAN
AT MIDDAY BLUE APPLES

The second parchment deciphered

This translation has baffled many but some have gained a little knowledge from it. The easy part is that SHEPHERDESS relates to the painting by Nicolas Poussin, ET IN ARCADIA EGO which we also found on the grave stone of Dame Marie de NEGRE D'ABLES. NO TEMPTATION refers to a painting by Teniers. The code clearly states these paintings HOLD THE KEY. Now for the rest which is quite simple to read with one adjustment. PEACE 681 is 189 reversed directing us to the date on the Visigoth CROSS 1891 outside the Church Mary Magdalene.

AND THIS HORSE OF GOD should read AND THIS HOUSE OF GOD meaning Mary Magdalene Church. I COMPLETE THIS DAEMON GUARDIAN is the demon statue Saunière put inside the Church as part of his renovation. AT MIDDAY BLUE APPLES are the small lights reflected through the stained glass windows of his Church.

SHEPHERDESS

A Painting by Nicolas Poussin SHEPHERDS OF ARCARDIA

ET IN ARCADIA EGO the inscription on the tomb of the painting by Nicolas Poussin 1638

The translation of the phrase is "Even in Arcadia, there am I".

NO TEMPTATION

We must also examine Tenier's TEMPTATION.

David Teniers's painting The Temptation of St Anthony

PEACE 681 BY THE CROSS

The 6 is reversed to give 981 and reversed again to give 189

PEACE 189 BY THE CROSS

The Visigoth Cross inscribed MISSON 1891

Within this Visigoth pillar that stands outside the Church it is claimed Bérenger Saunière found the old parchments. It was placed in the garden with a statue of Mary placed on top and inscribed at the bottom with the inscription MISSION 1891.

POUSSIN

Nicolas Poussin

He (Poussin) and I discussed certain things, which I shall with ease be able to explain to you in detail —things which will give you, through Monsieur Poussin, advantages which even kings would have great pains to draw from him, and which, according to him, it is possible that nobody else will ever discover in the centuries to come. And what is more, these are things so difficult to discover that nothing now on this earth can prove of better fortune be their equal'

The letter was first published by Anatole de Montaiglon in his book archives de l'Art francais 1862.

TENIERS

David Teniers the Younger or David Teniers II (15 December 1610 – 25 April 1690) was a Flemish painter, printmaker, draughtsman, miniaturist painter, copyist and art curator. He was an extremely versatile artist known for his prolific output.

HOLD THE KEY

SHEPHERDESS relates to the painting by Nicolas Poussin, ET IN ARCADIA EGO which we also found on the grave stone of Dame Marie de NEGRE D'ABLES. NO TEMPTATION refers to a painting by Teniers. The code clearly states these paintings HOLD THE KEY.

SHEPHERDESS

We already know the key shape is the Pentacle we will draw the Pentacle over the above painting since it is its basic geometry. I will draw each line until the very last which gives us a location.

NO TEMPTATION

David Teniers's painting The Temptation of St Anthony will help us in locating the exact spot for the treasure.

THIS HORSE OF GOD

The decipher gives THIS HORSE OF GOD, I believe this is a mistake in deciphering it should read THIS HOUSE OF GOD.

Mary Magdalene Church

The Latin inscription *Terribilis est locus iste* above the front doors, taken from the Common Dedication of a Church, which translates as: "This is a place of awe"; the rest of the dedication reads "this is God's house, the gate of heaven, and it shall be called the royal court of God."

I COMPLETE THIS DAEMON GUARDIAN

Figure at entrance of Mary Magdalene Church

(Make a note of hand gesture)

AT MIDDAY BLUE APPLES

Every 17th January these lights (Blue Apples) are seen inside
Mary Magdalene Church they are formed by an anomaly of
sunlight passing through the Church stained glass windows.

We must now put all the clues together and personally, I believe the second parchment and possibly the first parchment were made by Saunière himself. How else when decoded does it give the cipher 681 BY THE CROSS and when the number reversed 189(1) the year Saunière had inscribed on the Visigoth Cross. If we follow the clues in the second parchment they just lead us back to Mary Magdalene Church where resides the grave of Marie de Nègre d'Ables. It's almost like going around in circles. Even so, if he created the parchments he was certainly not responsible for the inscription on Marie de Nègre d'Ables gravestone which he defaced. So it is certain there he found the real clues to a secret, while possibly leaving others his ciphers.

What was the secret that Saunière knew? Why did he have written in Latin *Terribilis est locus iste* above his Church door? Was there some terrible secret inside? Why did he desecrate the grave of the noble lady Marie de Nègre d'Ables? Did he realize she knew a terrible secret and had it coded on her gravestone? Was this secret very harmful to the Church? Can the secret be the body of the KING is in fact Jesus and he was buried there?

It is conjecture of course, there is so much we do not know, all we can do is put the clues together. We are not even sure what we will find there are so many things unsure about this mystery. But our departure from this merry go round will be found in the paintings of Poussin and Teniers. These paintings hold the key.

ET IN ARCADIA EGO

In geometry like mathematics there is certainty and something tangible, a reality that enables one to get to grips with the truth. **We already know the key shape is the Pentacle we will draw the Pentacle over the Poussin painting since it is** its basic geometry. I will draw each line until the very last which gives us a location.

rock

The tomb of Arcadia and Rocher Noir in the background at Rennes-le-Château

All the clues if that's what they are point to this location on the hillside of Rennes-le-Château. The rock is seen in the painting of Poussin above his tomb.

The tomb of Arcadia and Rocher Noir seen on the hilly peak at Rennes-le-Château

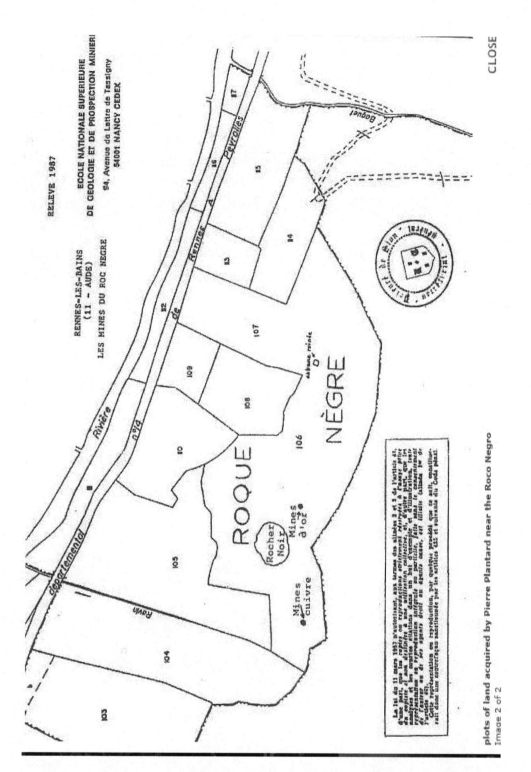

Map showing Rocher Noir (Black Rock) the plots of land
bought by Pierre Plantard

We are given one more clue in the mystery it is found in the translation of parchment two.

SHEPHERDESS NO TEMPTATION

TO WHICH POUSSIN TENNIERS HOLD THE KEY

We have dwelt with the painting of Poussin's SHEPHERDS OF ARCARDIA now we must examine Tennier's TEMPTATION.

David Teniers's painting The Temptation of St Anthony

The hut stands out also there is a woman that points to caves

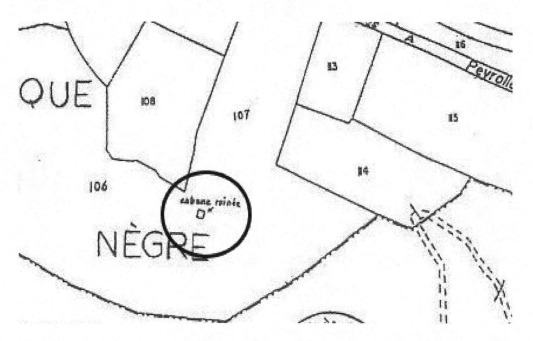

Cabane Rainie a WATER HUT. We are on the right track.

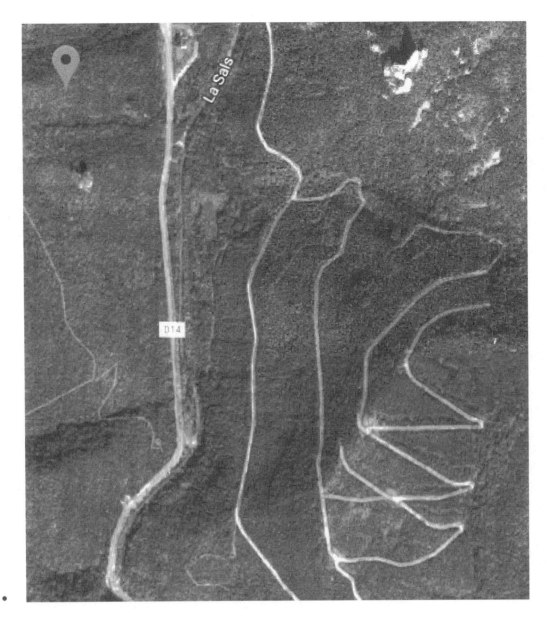

Surrounding area of Roque Negre

This is a large area and it is like finding a needle in a haystack but we are given some more help from the second parchment.

Where do we go from here?

We are nearing our destination, pinpointing the exact location for the treasure of the Knights Templar's. Now bear in mind few have come this close to solving the mystery sure some will draw pentacles across the country side and philosophise something is bigger here than treasure but that comes from the mouth of him who has failed to find treasure become reconciled to the fact he has become part of the mystery. At the end of the day it takes an outsider to see the wood through the trees to solve this mystery.

This strange insignia on the second parchment appears to be an old road configuration a clue that gives us a location (see below) We match the second parchment insignia with a location on the a map of Roque Negre this gives us the location next to La Sals.

To the right La Sals (IS) and to the left the location of the mine

Finally we are near the end of our journey with a pinpoint to the exact location where the mine is located. What is within we still don't know. We have to take seriously the thought that Saunière encapsulated this location in his renovations, garden layout and buildings and other works such as the placement of a grotto. I believe his estate layout is a mirror image of the above location.

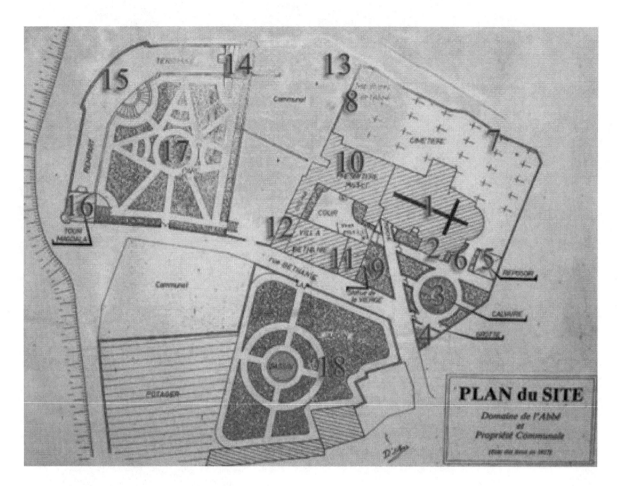

Plan of **Saunière's** estate layout

1. Church of Mary Magdalene
2. Sacrristie
3. Calvaire
4. Grotto
5. Reposoir
6. Cementry Gate
7. Ossarium
8. Original tomb of Sauniere
9. Notre Dame d Lourdes
10. Presbytery
11. Villa Bethania
12. House Chapel
13. Sauniere tomb
14. Orangerie
15. Belvedere
16. Tour Magdala
17. Parc
18. Villa Gardens

XXSLX is a code inside Saunière's Grotto meaning (La Sals)

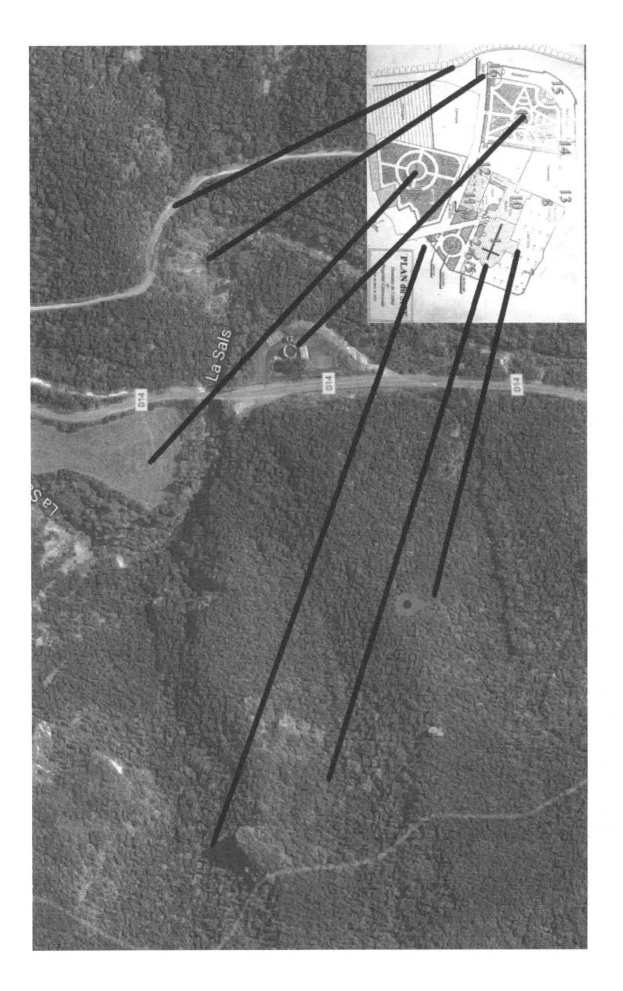

JESU. MEDELA. VULNERUM ✦ SPES. UNA. PŒNITENTIUM.
PER. MAGDALENÆ. LACRYMAS ✦ PECCATA. NOSTRA. DILUAS

The Altar of Mary Magdalene Church showing a base relief of
Mary Magdalene herself in a grotto next to a book and a skull.
She crosses her fingers an esoteric meaning she knows a great
secret. Mary Magdalene was a main witness to the crucifixion,
burial and resurrection of Jesus, she was a lead disciple and it is
claimed as a part of the Catharist belief that Jesus had a sexual
relationship with Mary Magdalene, described as his concubine.
The skull in the picture, who does it represent? Is it the skull of
Jesus? Is the secret we have found the location of the burial of
the dead body of Jesus carried and buried by Mary Magdalene?

REDIS REGIS CELLIS ARCHIS

REPEAT KING BODY DEAD

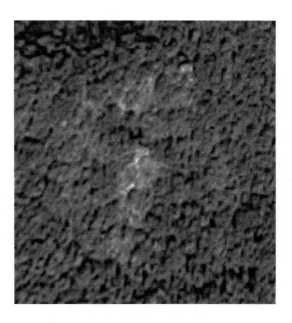

DAEMON GUARDIAN appears on the hill side

To get underneath the hill we have to enter the mine shaft and we are fortunate we have a photo of how the entrance appears. I can confirm this mine embodies the DAEMON GUARDIAN or guard we find symbolized on entry to Mary Magdalene Church.

View from inside the mine shaft.

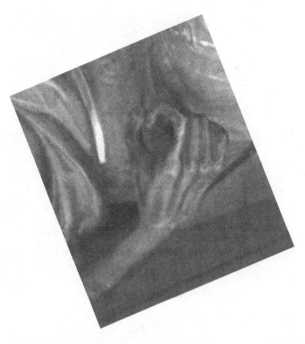

Compare the hand gesture with the mine shaft entrance
and remember where we found this!

DAEMON GUARDIAN

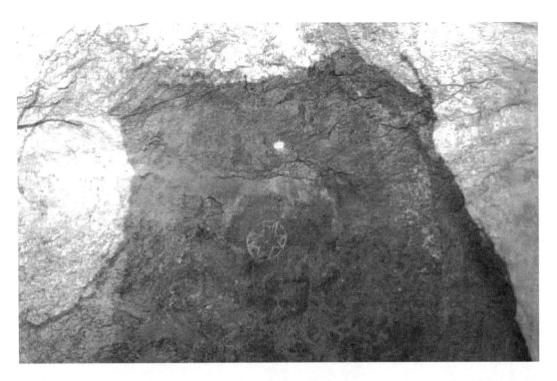

A Templar emblem inside the mine the eight pointed star

After entry into the mine it becomes very steep, in the chamber at the end of the tunnel on the wall is a vein of glittering pyrite. There is an eight pointed circle on the gallery wall greeting you. At the bottom of the shaft lead two opposing galleries these lead deep into the mountain, one tunnel has been blocked by debris.

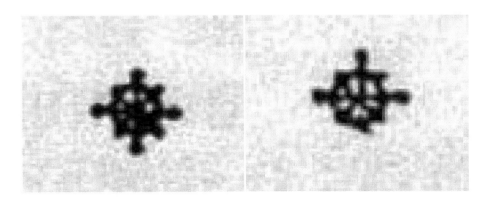

Templar emblem on parchment two

Engraved Templar emblem inside mine (Star of Bethlehem?)

This is clearest evidence yet that within these tunnels can be found something that is precious. We have been led to the location using, the Rennes-le-Château parchments and the correct deciphering of the inscription on the gravestone of Marie de Nègre d'Ables. These pictures were taken by a cave excavator not hunting for treasure or realizing the emblems significance therefore just made minimal entry into the mine.

In 2008 a Dutch researcher Klaas van Urk, author of *Search for the Holy Grail and the Ark of the Covenant* which was a best seller in the Netherlands, discovered a similar Templar sign in a narrow shaft hidden high on Mount Cardou high above the ridge from our mine. But access to this mine was impossible. A rope with a camera was fed down the narrow mine shaft. His finds confirms mine we are in the tunnels of the Templar's.

The eight pointed star is significant it is associated with Inanna the Mesopotamian **goddess** of love, beauty, sex, desire, fertility, war, justice, and political power. She was known as the "Queen of Heaven" She was associated with the planet Venus and her most prominent symbols included the **eight-pointed star.** Her myth relates to her being dragged into the underworld. The Templar's goddess could be her archetype Mary Magdalene.

The eight-pointed star was Inanna's most common symbol.

If we follow Sumerian mythology then we find that Inanna marries Tammuz. The cult of Ishtar and Tammuz continued to thrive until the eleventh century AD (time of the Knights Templar) and survived in parts of Mesopotamia as late as the eighteenth century. Tammuz is mentioned by name in the **Book of Ezekiel** and possibly alluded to in other passages from the **Hebrew Bible.** In late nineteenth and early twentieth century **scholarship of religion,** Tammuz was widely seen as a prime example of the **archetypal dying-and-rising god.**

Inanna and her consort Tammuz

Why did the knights Templar use Inanna's symbol the eight pointed star and associate itself with this Goddess? Does her mythology parallel a truth about Mary Magdalene and Jesus? Now we touch on the work of Henry Lincoln who claimed in his book *The Holy Blood and the Holy Grail* (1982) that Mary Magdalene was married to Jesus and had a child through him whose descendants were the founders of the Merovingian kings in the 5th century. A stream of works in our modern era, have based their thesis on this hypothesis but they were not the first. The 13th-century monk and chronicler Peter of Vaux de Cernay claimed it was part of Catharist belief that Jesus had a relationship with Mary Magdalene, described as his concubine.

I leave readers to ponder too make up their own mind whether we have discovered the hiding place of the lost treasures of the Templar's perhaps the Holy Grail or the Ark of the Covenant or maybe something more sacred, whatever the case maybe, only a thorough excavation of the mine will discover the hidden secret.

PART TWO
The Da Vinci Code

PART TWO

Scholars, researchers and experts alike all agree there is no such thing as a Da Vinci Code. In this work we shall reexamine the case and reveal my findings not the one sensationalized but one found in geometry revealing Leonardo's belief in the illuminati, discovery of which, will cast a new understanding upon his art.

"Mirror" Writing

Leonardo used "mirror" writing he wrote backwards and his notes could only be deciphered by holding up a mirror to obtain the meaning. It is unclear exactly why Leonardo did this. It is a very easy code to break to the determined code breaker so it seems this writing was used to confuse the casual observer. Some of his military designs and inventions he possibly wanted to keep out of the hands of powerful people or out of the hands of destructive individuals, or his code was a means of retaining copyright. Many have put forth the proposition that he used "mirror" writing because he found it easier. He was naturally left-handed and this would have made writing backwards easy.

Mona Lisa

It would be true to suggest that he did paint secret symbols and numbers in his artwork. Most people that view his Mona Lisa are drawn to her smile which when viewed at different angles seems to broaden. A technique Leonardo used was to paint the edges off her mouth her smile slightly out of focus to obtain this effect. However, when her eyes are viewed under a microscope, these eyes of "Mona Lisa" are containing numbers and letters.

So what is the Mona Lisa smiling about?

The Last Supper

The Last Supper painting depicts the last Passover meal before the death of Jesus. Leonardo attempts to capture that poignant moment when Jesus announces at the table he is about to be betrayed. The composition actually is based on events described by St John in the Gospel. According to Dan Brown's book the disciple sitting to the right of Jesus usually identified as St John is actually the woman Mary Magdalene. This leads us to the big conspiracy secret that Jesus was married to Mary Magdalene.

Indeed, a first glance at the painting seems to confirm this. The disciple to Jesus' right that swoons like a woman has long hair and smooth skin with what might be looked upon as feminine features compared to the rougher-looking disciples at the table.

The sensationalist theory takes this as evidence that Leonardo painted a young woman, rather than a man. Some indicate that Jesus and the figure to his right are painted forming a 'V' shape representing a womb making homage to the "divine feminine." Also tracing lines for the shape of Jesus and the feminine figure to his right are said to form the shape of the letter "M," perhaps.

These of course are sensationalizing theories but the painting itself does draw us to the conclusion that some kind of message is contained within the composition. "As we look at the painting we ask why he chose those particular foods, because they don't correspond to what the narrative described," "Why bread, salt, fish, citrus and wine? Why is the saltshaker tipped over in front of Judas? Why is the bread leavened?" It was the Jewish custom to always eat unleavened bread, bread without yeast and back to the sensationalist theory, why does John look like a woman? In this work we are going to examine those clues and reveal the secret symmetry the masters used to reveal hidden knowledge.

The Last Supper chronicles a major event in the life of Jesus the evening before he was betrayed by Judas it is his final meal.

The Last Supper based on scripture

John 13:21 "After Jesus had said these things he was deeply troubled and told his disciples, 'I tell you for certain that one of you will betray me'"

A casual observer of the painting of The Last Supper would first observe the figure of Christ as central and prominent in the picture. A more enlightened individual would notice that the figures sat around the table are painted without halos signifying men who are down to earth. A person with a biblical mindset and an eye for detail would be confounded by the oddity of daylight emanating from the window behind Christ suggesting the meal took place during the day but the biblical narrative it states, the Last Supper took place at night. Why did Leonardo depict the outside scenery during the day showing hazy light outside through the windows? An art scholar would suggest it all just a case of artistic license having no meanings attached or derived from it. But Leonardo was a man who depicted the truth and he would've followed the narrative of his subject closely, after all he was mandated to paint a true representation and no doubt his commission would've depended upon it.

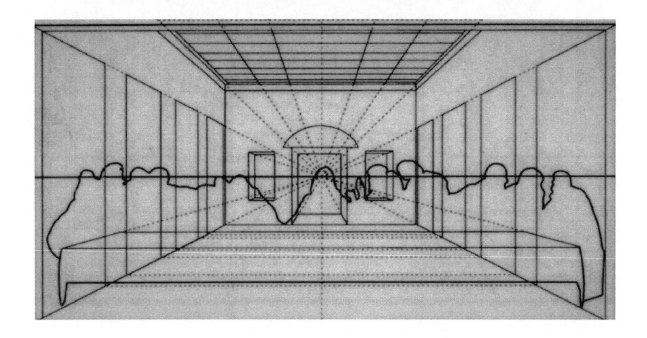

Da Vinci was well known for his love of symmetry his painting of the Last Supper is largely horizontal. The front table is seen in the foreground of the image with all of the subjects behind it. His first thoughts on the painting lies in the notes that he made concerning the effects of light and shadow that was found in a manuscript he was writing during the Last Supper. By placing a lighted candle behind him the shadow produced was drawn over on the canvas. This manuscript shows his first thoughts on the main figure for Christ based on himself his own shadow.

The painting depicts the last Passover meal before the death of Jesus. Leonardo attempts to capture that poignant moment when Jesus announces at the table he is about to be betrayed by one of his disciples. The composition actually is based on events described by St John in the Gospel.

A casual observer of the painting of The Last Supper would first observe the figure of Christ as central and prominent in the picture. A more enlightened individual would notice that the figures sat around the table are painted without halos signifying men who are down to earth. A person with a biblical mindset and an eye for detail would be confounded by the oddity of daylight emanating from the window behind Christ suggesting the meal took place during the day but the biblical narrative it states, the Last Supper took place at night. The Code to the masterpiece lies in the notes that Leonardo made concerning light and shadow found in a manuscript he was writing during his composition of the Last Supper. By placing a lighted candle behind him the shadow produced was drawn over on the canvas. This manuscript shows his first thoughts on the figure for Christ based on himself his own shadow.

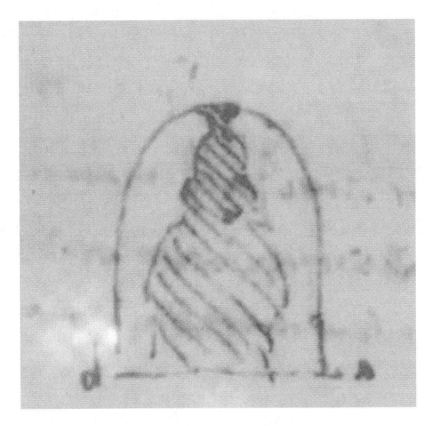

Image from his notes on light and shadow

Leonardo's drawing transcribed over the image of Christ

Investigating *The Last Supper* we can be certain and state that Leonardo based the figure of Christ on his own shadow a self representation. The question now is how did, he proceed, for the rest of the composition what means were at to his disposal for him to construct a painting of himself in conjunction with the personages of the gospel. This question would be answered through the art of astrology. A serious form of study during the renaissance when Leonardo was alive and he would've known that a horoscope of his birth was his own shadow in a celestial form. A birth chart shows the position of the planets and houses at the moment of birth along with the celestial dynamics good and bad that are made between the planetary orbs at that moment. To introduce the reader to this we need to reveal the birth chart of Leonardo and compare it to the picture layout of The Last Supper. We begin by knowing his birth time the third hour of the night 15 April, 1452. His birth chart below shows the position of his planets the 12 houses.

It has to be noted finding the correct time of birth for earlier centuries can be difficult, and times given are often unreliable since sources can vary. However, records state that Leonardo was born at the *"Third hour of the night"* Renaissance time – that is, three hours after the last *"Ave Maria"* – which most biographers seem to agree on (Lois Rodden, gives 9.40p.m. birth) giving 6 degrees of Sagittarius on the Ascendant with Neptune conjunct the MC.

Science is the observation of things possible, whether present or past; prescience is the knowledge of things which may come to pass, though but slowly.

Leonardo da Vinci

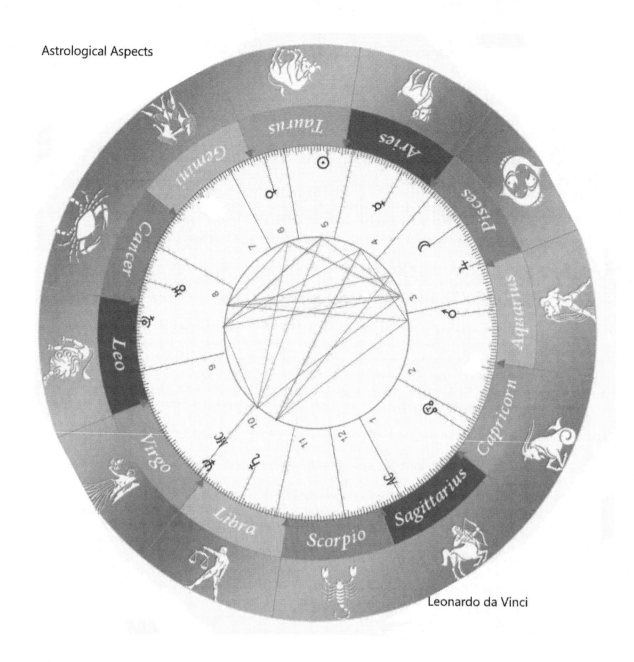

Leonardo da Vinci

The Birth Chart of Leonardo da Vinci

John and Jesus

The Sun or Jesus

The sun is in the 5th house and Venus is in the 6th house in the Birth Chart of Leonardo da Vinci their position makes astrological aspects (degree distance) to the other planets and when these aspects are drawn we get the characteristic ´V´ shape between Jesus and John in the painting composition. This suggests Leonardo is using the aspects in his chart to draft his masterpiece identifying the sun with the presence of Jesus and Venus with his disciple John. This discovery will enable us to unravel a mystery which has remained hidden to Church and art historian alike. What made Leonardo draw the ´V´ shape into his painting so dramatically.

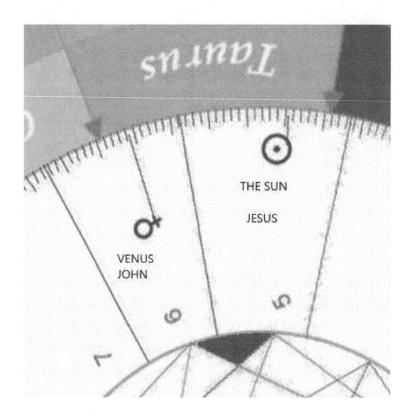

The Sun and Venus in the Birth Chart of Leonardo with the characteristic ´V' shape found in his aspects which he used as a frame work for art, the sun to represent Jesus and Venus John.

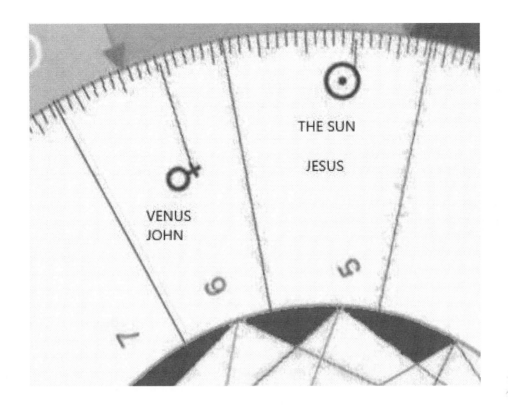

THE SUN

JESUS

VENUS
JOHN

The shape of Jesus and the mysterious figure to His right are said to form the shape of the letter "M," by tracing the shape formed by the astrological aspects we get the composition. Leonardo balanced the perspective construction of the Last Supper so that its vanishing point is immediately behind Christ's right temple, pointing to the physical location of the centre, or sensus communis, of his brain. By pulling a string in radial directions from this point, he marked the positions of the right hand of Jesus, the citrus and the left hand of Jesus and by pulling a string from the temple of James and John he pointed to the citrus in front of Jesus.

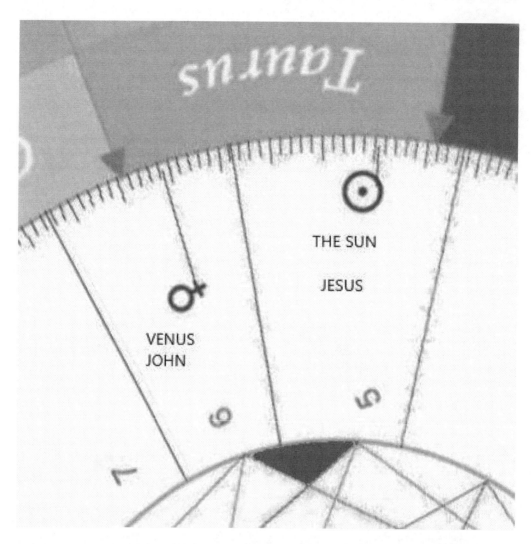

Astrological aspects lines showing ´V' shape

The symmetry lines are the same for the aspect lines and they mark the position of the planets in the birth chart of Leonardo

Leonardo has based his painting of The Last Supper on his own Birth Chart and his understanding of astrology this is a glimpse into his theory on the relationships between himself and Christ. We can carry this theory further and apply the Major and Minor astrological aspects in his Chart with the apostles themselves who are showing their reaction to a secret teaching given at the Last Supper. Firstly, the reader is introduced into the meaning of the astrological aspects. This information is given below:

Major Aspects

In astrology, an aspect is an angle the planets make to each other in the horoscope, also to the ascendant, midheaven,

descendant, lower midheaven, and other points
of astrological interest.

The traditional major aspects are sometimes called *Ptolemaic aspects* since they were defined and used by Ptolemy in the 1st Century, AD. These aspects are the conjunction (0°), sextile (60°), square (90°), trine (120°), and opposition (180°). It is important to note that different astrologers and separate astrological systems/traditional utilize differing *orbs* (the degree of separation between exactitude) when calculating and using the aspects, though almost all use a larger orb for a conjunction when compared to the other aspects. The major aspects are those that can be used to divide 360 evenly and are divisible by 10 (with the exception of the semi-sextile).

Conjunction

A conjunction is an angle of approximately 0-10°. An orb of approximately 10° is usually considered a conjunction, however if neither the Sun or Moon is involved, some consider the conjunction to have a maximum distance of only about 0±08°. This is said to be the most powerful aspect, intensifying the effects of the involved planets mutually — and being a major point in the chart.

Whether the union is to be regarded as "positive" or "negative" depends upon what planets are involved: Venus, Jupiter and the Sun, in any possible combination, is considered the most favourable scenario (and all three actually met on November 9–10, 1970, for example), while the most unfavourable configurations involve Mars, Saturn, and/or the Moon (with all three conjoining on March 10 in that same year). If the planets are under stress from other configurations, then the conjunction will be said to intensify the stress. When a planet is in *very* close conjunction to the Sun it is referred to as cazimi;

when a planet is moderately close to the Sun, it is said to be combust. The Sun and Moon are in conjunction monthly during the New Moon.

Sextile — intermediate major/minor aspect

A sextile is an angle of 60° (1/6 of the 360° ecliptic, or 1/2 of a trine [120°]). A separation (orb) of 60° is considered a sextile. An orb between 3-4 is allowed depending on the planets involved. The sextile has been traditionally said to be similar in influence to the trine, but less intense. It indicates ease of communication between the two elements involved, with compatibility and harmony between them. A sextile provides opportunity and is very responsive to effort expended to gain its benefits. See information on the *semisextile* below.

Square

A square is an angle of 90° (1/4 of the 360° ecliptic, or 1/2 of an opposition [180°]). An orb of somewhere between 5° and 10°[3] is usually allowed depending on the planets involved. As with the trine and the sextile, in the square, it is usually the outer or superior planet that has an effect on the inner or inferior one. The square's energy is strong and usable but has a tension that needs integration between 2 different areas of life, or offers a choice point where an important decision needs to be made that involves an opportunity cost. It is the smallest major aspect that usually involves houses in different quadrants.

Trine

A trine is an angle of 120° (1/3 of the 360° ecliptic), an orb of somewhere between 5° and 10° depending on the planets involved. The trine relates to what is natural and indicates harmony and ease. The trine may involve talent or ability which is innate. The trine has been traditionally assumed to be extremely beneficial. When involved in a transit, the trine involves situations that emerge from a current or past situation in a natural way.

Opposition

An opposition is an angle of 180° (1/2 of the 360° ecliptic). An orb of somewhere between 5° and 10° is usually allowed depending on the planets. Oppositions are said to be the second most powerful aspect. It resembles the conjunction although the difference between them is that the opposition is fundamentally relational. Some say it is prone to exaggeration as it is not unifying like the conjunction but has a dichotomous quality and an externalizing effect. All important axes in astrology are essentially oppositions. Therefore, at its most basic, it often signifies a relationship that can be oppositional or complementary.

John

The symbol of Venus or John

Venus is the Goddess of love essentially associated with the feminine and is the astrological ruler of Taurus and Libra. A planet that symbolises beauty and has ruler ship over the throat in anatomy (Peter touches the throat of John). Its metal is red copper hence the cape colour of John. This identification of the position of Venus in the painting of Leonardo emphasises but does not prove that the figure drawn is indeed a young woman.

But adds weight to the theory found in the DaVinci Code that this figure is based on the feminine Venus, Mary Magdalene.

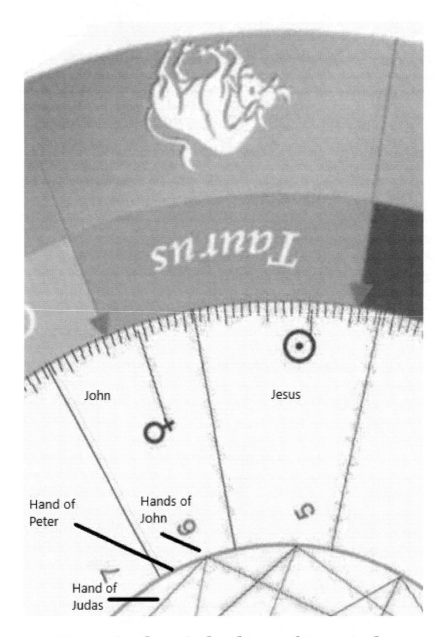

Venus in the Birth Chart of Leonardo

Peter and Judas

The Symbol for Pluto or Peter

Peter holds a knife symbolising death (Pluto is the Lord of Death) and he leans over the shoulder of Judas and questions John.

The symbol for Uranus or Judas

Judas clasps his bag of silver while knocking over a small circular container of salt. Many scholars have discussed the meaning of the spilled salt container near Judas's elbow. Spilled salt here SYMBOLISING the glyph of Uranus. Judas sits next to John this is symbolic for the 60 degree aspect of Uranus to Venus separated by the seventh house of hidden enemies.

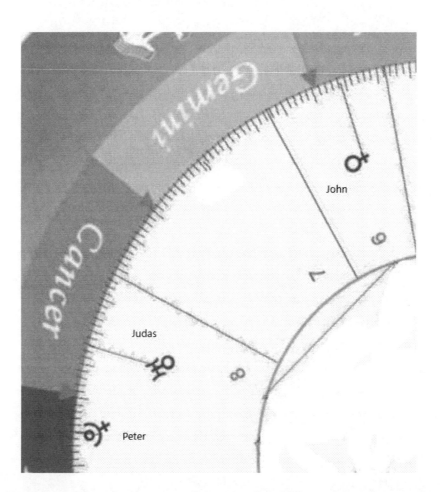

Pluto and Uranus in the Birth Chart of Leonardo

James the Less and Andrew

The symbol for Neptune or James the Less

James the Less (Neptune) rests his left hand on the shoulder of
Peter (Pluto) this is symbolic for the 60 degree aspect of
Neptune to Pluto in the Birth Chart of Leonardo.

Mᶜ

The symbol for the mid heaven point or Andrew

In the composition we see James the Less (Neptune) putting his
hand on the shoulder of Andrew (MC) representing the
conjunction of Neptune with the MC in the Birth Chart.

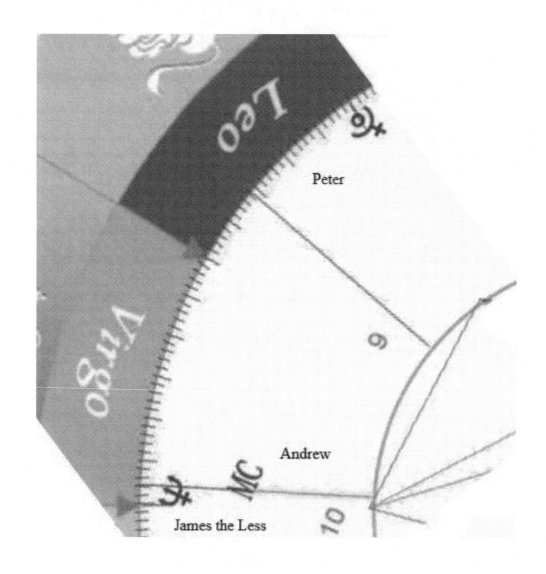

Neptune, MC and Pluto in the Birth Chart of Leonardo

Bartholomew

The symbol for Saturn or Bartholomew

Bartholomew points to the table cloth strips note also the knot above his cloak resembling the symbol for Saturn which is in Libra the 7th sign of the Zodiac in the Birth Chart of Leonardo.

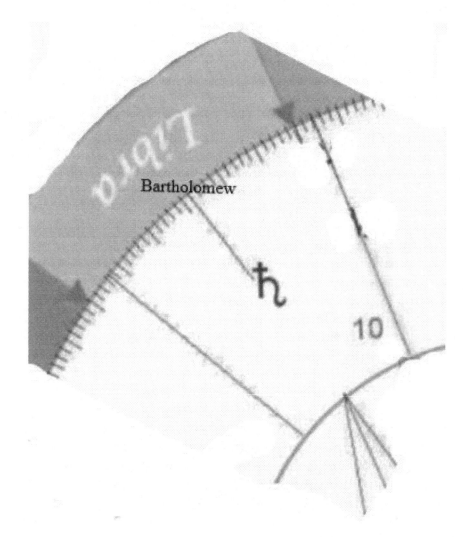

Saturn in the Birth Chart of Leonardo

Thomas and James Major

The symbol of Mercury or Thomas

Thomas points his one finger upwards designating the first sign of the Zodiac, Aries. Mercury is in Aries in the Birth Chart the orb is closer to the sun as Thomas is to Jesus in the painting.

The symbol of the Moon or James Major

James Major symbolising the Moon backs off letting Thomas representing Mercury take first place. In the Birth Chart Mercury is closer to the sun than the Moon. The Moon makes two wide aspects in the Birth Chart of Leonardo shown by the spread eagle arms of James Major.

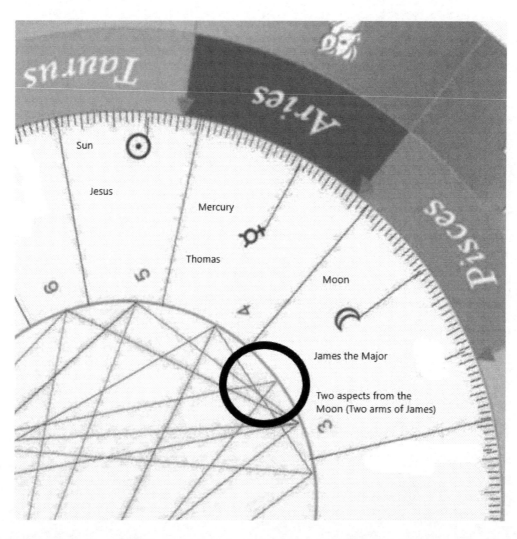

Mercury and the Moon in the Birth Chart of Leonardo

Phillip and Matthew

2

The symbol of Jupiter or Phillip

Of all the planets in the chart of Leonardo Jupiter is the most powerful since it makes the most aspects to the other planets a total of five and Phillip symbolises this total by having five hands drawn in his body area.

The symbol of Mars or Matthew

The Apostle by his expression of his arms emphasises the point of the symbol for Mars

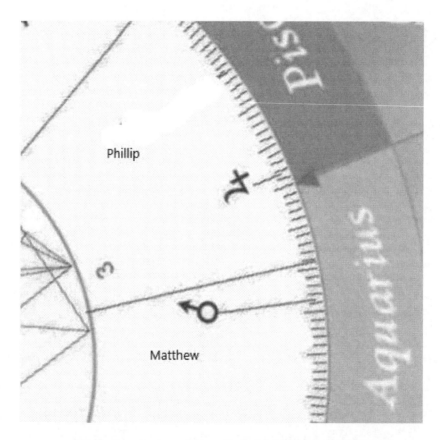

Jupiter and Mars in the Birth Chart of Leonardo

Thaddeus and Simon

True Lunar Node

The symbol for True Lunar Node or Thaddeus

Thaddeus makes a gesture with his left hand an upside down T. Note also Simon has the fullest beard of the Apostles the North Node is in the sign of the goat (Beard).

A^{SC}

The symbol for the Ascendant or Simon

The Ascendant represents the distinctive appearance of a person and Simon is the only bald headed Apostle

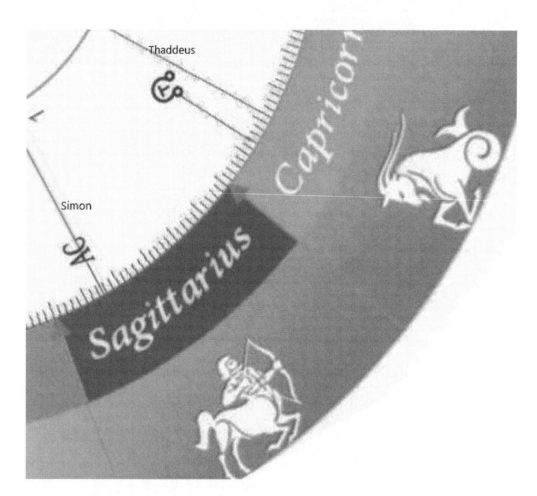

North Node and Ascendant in the Birth Chart of Leonardo

The masterpiece contains a number of allusions to the number 3, (symbolizing the Holy Trinity the Spirit). The disciples are seated in four groups of three; there are three windows, while the figure of Jesus himself is given a triangular shape, marked by his head and two outstretched arms. The picture depicts the reaction of each disciple to the news of the betrayal of Jesus. But there is no Scriptural basis on how each disciple took the news Leonardo is free to emulate each emotion with artistic license. Why are they all reacting so differently, some with surprise, some look angry, some shocked and taken aback while some look for an answer to the question, it looks like a fierce debate about his secret teachings not about who betrays him.

GROUP 1
Bartholomew, James the Less and Andrew are all surprised.

• GROUP 2
Judas Iscariot is taken aback; next to him, Peter holds a knife and looks stormy, while the John, the youngest apostle, swoons.

• GROUP 3
Thomas is upset; James is shocked. Philip wants an explanation.

• GROUP 4
Jude Thaddeus and Matthew turn to Simon the Zealot for answers.

Peter holds a knife and looks stormy

1. And he said, "Whoever discovers the interpretation of these sayings will not taste death."

2. Jesus said, "Those who seek should not stop seeking until they find. When they find, they will be disturbed. When they are disturbed, they will marvel, and will reign over all. [And after they have reigned they will rest.]"

Philip wants an explanation.

3. Jesus said, "If your leaders say to you, 'Look, the (Father's) kingdom is in the sky,' then the birds of the sky will precede you. If they say to you, 'It is in the sea,' then the fish will precede you. Rather, the (Father's) kingdom is within you and it is outside you.

When you know yourselves, then you will be known, and you will understand that you are children of the living Father. But if you do not know yourselves, then you live in poverty, and you are the poverty."

James the Less is surprised

4. Jesus said, "The person old in days won't hesitate to ask a little child seven days old about the place of life, and that person will live.

For many of the first will be last, and will become a single one."

John, the youngest apostle, swoons

5. Jesus said, "Know what is in front of your face, and what is hidden from you will be disclosed to you.

For there is nothing hidden that will not be revealed. [And there is nothing buried that will not be raised.]"

Judas Iscariot is taken aback

6. His disciples asked him and said to him, "Do you want us to fast? How should we pray? Should we give to charity? What diet should we observe?"

Jesus said, "Don't lie, and don't do what you hate, because all things are disclosed before heaven. After all, there is nothing hidden that will not be revealed, and there is nothing covered up that will remain undisclosed."

Philip wants an explanation.

"Lord, show us the Father, and it is enough for us." Jesus answered, "Don't you know me, Philip, even after I have been among you such a long time? Anyone who has seen me has seen the Father. How can you say, 'Show us the Father'? (John 14:9)

John, the youngest apostle, swoons

7. Jesus said, "Lucky is the lion that the human will eat, so that the lion becomes human. And foul is the human that the lion will eat, and the lion still will become human."

8. And he said, "The person is like a wise fisherman who cast his net into the sea and drew it up from the sea full of little fish. Among them the wise fisherman discovered a fine large fish. He threw all the little fish back into the sea, and easily chose the large fish. Anyone here with two good ears had better listen!"

James the Less is surprised

9. Jesus said, "Look, the sower went out, took a handful (of seeds), and scattered (them). Some fell on the road, and the birds came and gathered them. Others fell on rock, and they didn't take root in the soil and didn't produce heads of grain. Others fell on thorns, and they choked the seeds and worms ate them. And others fell on good soil, and it produced a good crop: it yielded sixty per measure and one hundred twenty per measure."

Andrew is surprised

10. Jesus said, "I have cast fire upon the world, and look, I'm guarding it until it blazes."

John, the youngest apostle, swoons

11. Jesus said, "This heaven will pass away, and the one above it will pass away.

The dead are not alive, and the living will not die. During the days when you ate what is dead, you made it come alive. When you are in the light, what will you do? On the day when you were one, you became two. But when you become two, what will you do?"

Judas Iscariot is taken aback

12. The disciples said to Jesus, "We know that you are going to leave us. Who will be our leader?"

James is shocked

Jesus said to them, "No matter where you are you are to go to James the Just, for whose sake heaven and earth came into being."

Thomas is upset

13. Jesus said to his disciples, "Compare me to something and tell me what I am like."

Simon Peter said to him, "You are like a just messenger."

Matthew said to him, "You are like a wise philosopher."

Thomas said to him, "Teacher, my mouth is utterly unable to say what you are like."

Jesus said, "I am not your teacher. Because you have drunk, you have become intoxicated from the bubbling spring that I have tended."

And he took him, and withdrew, and spoke three sayings to him.

Peter holds a knife and looks stormy

When Thomas came back to his friends they asked him, "What did Jesus say to you?"

Thomas said to them, "If I tell you one of the sayings he spoke to me, you will pick up rocks and stone me, and fire will come from the rocks and devour you."

Matthew turns to Simon the Zealot for answers.

14. Jesus said to them, "If you fast, you will bring sin upon yourselves, and if you pray, you will be condemned, and if you give to charity, you will harm your spirits.

Judas Iscariot is taken aback

When you go into any region and walk about in the countryside, when people take you in, eat what they serve you and heal the sick among them.

After all, what goes into your mouth will not defile you; rather, it's what comes out of your mouth that will defile you."

James the Less is surprised

15. Jesus said, "When you see one who was not born of woman, fall on your faces and worship. That one is your Father."

Peter holds a knife and looks stormy

16. Jesus said, "Perhaps people think that I have come to cast peace upon the world. They do not know that I have come to cast conflicts upon the earth: fire, sword, war.

For there will be five in a house: there'll be three against two and two against three, father against son and son against father, and they will stand alone."

17. Jesus said, "I will give you what no eye has seen, what no ear has heard, what no hand has touched, what has not arisen in the human heart."

Philip wants an explanation.

18. The disciples said to Jesus, "Tell us, how will our end come?"

Jesus said, "Have you found the beginning, then, that you are looking for the end? You see, the end will be where the beginning is.

Congratulations to the one who stands at the beginning: that one will know the end and will not taste death."

Peter holds a knife and looks stormy

19. Jesus said, "Congratulations to the one who came into being before coming into being.

If you become my disciples and pay attention to my sayings, these stones will serve you.

For there are five trees in Paradise for you; they do not change, summer or winter, and their leaves do not fall. Whoever knows them will not taste death."

Andrew and James are both surprised

20. The disciples said to Jesus, "Tell us what Heaven's kingdom is like."

He said to them, "It's like a mustard seed, the smallest of all seeds, but when it falls on prepared soil, it produces a large plant and becomes a shelter for birds of the sky."

Leonardo knew the position of the five known planets along with the Sun and Moon MC, AC and North Node in his Chart.

> Science is the observation of things possible, whether present or past; prescience is the knowledge of things which may come to pass, though but slowly.

> Leonardo da Vinci

There can be no doubt that Leonardo used his own astrological birth chart to compose the Last Supper. Based on the aspects in his chart he drew lines from Christ and the apostles to line up with the items on the table. The question is why? Why did he feel a need to base the Son of God on his own birth chart, what was his belief system that identified himself to Christ. Research of the heretical beliefs at the time of Leonardo reveal a mystical form of Christianity did emerge during his period called the Illuminato, plural Illuminati, a heretical group born in Italy, its adherents claimed that the human soul, having reached a high degree of perfection could achieve union with GOD the soul illumined by the Holy Spirit. Consequently, worship, and the observance of exterior forms of religion such as the reception of the sacraments as advocated by the Catholic Church was unnecessary for salvation. Also the soul on reception of the Spirit could neither advance beyond that point nor regress because the soul had received the "light." Therefore persons in this state of perfection could indulge their sexual desires and commit other sinful acts freely without staining their souls. In essence it was a belief based on Gnosis. *Gnosis* refers to knowledge based on personal experience or perception.

"Although I cannot quote from authors in the same way they do, I shall rely on a much worthier thing, actual experience, which is the only thing that could ever have properly guided the men that they learn from."

From the note books of Leonardo da Vinci

"I am well aware that because I did not study the ancients, some foolish men will accuse me of being uneducated. They will say that because I did not learn from their schoolbooks, I am unqualified to express an opinion. But I would reply that my conclusions are drawn from firsthand experience, unlike the scholars who only believe what they read in books written by others."

From the note books of Leonardo da Vinci

The beliefs of the Illuminati would also appeal to Leonardo for he was by sexual persuasion Gay which the Illuminati tolerated.

In 1476, Leonardo da Vinci, on the verge of his twenty-fourth birthday, was named as one of four men who had practiced "such wickedness" with the seventeen-year-old apprentice of a local goldsmith. He was arrested and possibly spent time in jail, but his case got dismissed through lack of witnesses. If he had been found guilty it would've of meant either a large fine, exile or even burning at the stake, for such acts were deemed illegal by the government of Florence during the Renaissance.

So we are dealing with the belief system of the Illuminati. It should be noted that their beliefs were carried over by the Freemasons in the 17th century and the Rosicrucian's around the same time a belief that its members possess secret wisdom.

Leonardo has already demonstrated he has a full understanding of the astrological science we must now look at his painting in greater detail by lining up the symmetry and here we find in its detail a picture within a picture the basis of his Illuminati belief.

Extending the lines of the symmetry we form a pyramid.

Many have appreciated and recognized that the Great Pyramid contains numerous scientific truths, but it is not so generally known that this ancient edifice is referred to in the Bible, and few realize that the biblical plan of salvation is corroborated by the *symbolisms* of the building. Jesus alluded to this symbolism when addressing the rulers of Israel:

"Did ye never read in the Scriptures, The stone which the builders rejected, the same is become the head of the corner: this is the Lord's doing, and it is marvelous in our eyes?"

(Matt. 21:42).

Since Leonardo has identified the Great Pyramid with his birth chart could he in fact be telling us that this edifice is a star chart in stone? This leaves us with the thought the Illuminati believed for it was known as the stone of 'Light' from the ancient of days.

Thus design of the Pyramid is based on mans illumination, and the position of the planets in a chart in the solar system during birth in Spirit. Leonardo was the most illumined man of his age thus why not base painting of the Last Supper on his own chart.

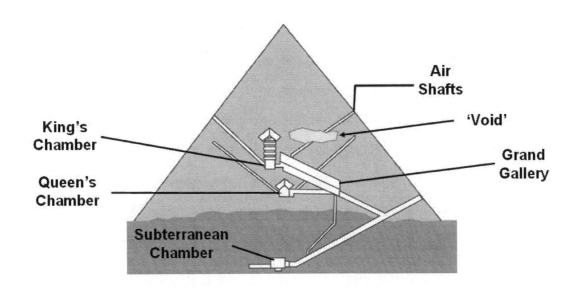

The extended symmetry of the Last Supper appears to resemble major points in the design of the Great Pyramid. Is it possible that the Subterranean Chamber level be identified with the area beneath the table of the Last Supper? The Kings Chamber with the position of Jesus and the outstretched arm of Jesus with the Grand Gallery? The position of the Queens Chamber with the position of the platter in front of Jesus and the extended lines that form in the symmetry of the painting with the Air Shafts? Lastly, the pointed finger of Thomas shows the position of the Void, is it the location of an important artifact the Holy Grail? All this is conjecture of course nevertheless an interesting idea.

Symbolism with the Great Pyramid

Jesus – king's Chamber

From the head of Jesus – The air shaft of the king's Chamber

The large plate or Holy Grail – Queen's Chamber

The pointing finger of Thomas- The void in the Great Pyramid

Left arm of Jesus – Grand Gallery

From the head of John – Queen's Chamber air shaft

From the head of James – Queen's Chamber air shaft

Underneath the table – The Subterranean Chamber

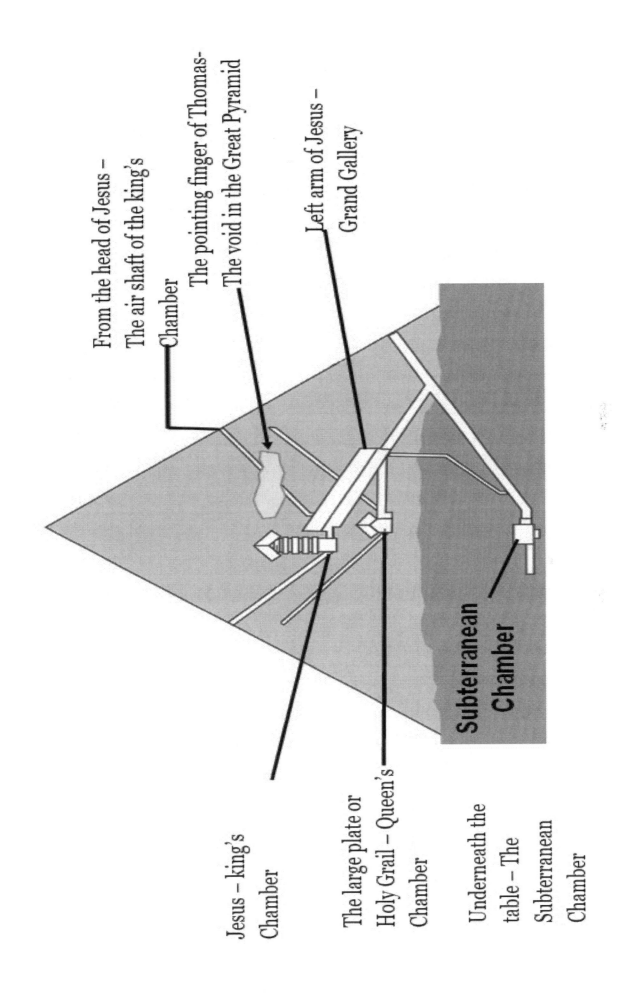

From the head of Jesus –
The air shaft of the king's
Chamber

The pointing finger of Thomas-
The void in the Great Pyramid

Left arm of Jesus –
Grand Gallery

Jesus – king's
Chamber

The large plate or
Holy Grail – Queen's
Chamber

Underneath the
table – The
Subterranean
Chamber

Subterranean
Chamber

Shepherds of Acadia 1637

Later mystical painters like Nicolas Poussin have also referred to a mystical stone. In the Shepherds of Acadia for instance 'Et in Arcadia Ego' is inscribed in the centre of the tomb and translated as "the person buried in this tomb lived in Arcadia." Arcadia is euphemism for heaven. The mystery surrounding the painting is found through the subjects that surround it for they are symbols for the planets and signs at a given time. They are as follows the Shepherdess (Cancer), young man (Mars), figure wearing beard (Jupiter) and finally Saturn. The shadow that the arm forms is indicating the crescent Moon phase. The Moon rules Cancer (Shepherdess) hence is being shown her position. A mystery revealed through spiritual experience these being the positions of the planets the moment a person unifies with spirit. During realisation the light of the orbs filters through the rising sign of Aquarius (the urn) that rises in the east at that moment.

Nicolas Poussin's painting The Shepherds of Arcadia

APPENDIX

Bérenger Saunière

Marie Denarnaud was the maid and confidant of Saunière

André GALAUP

Bérenger Saunière and village friends

Mary Magdalene Church

Bérenger Saunière in the grounds of his Villa Bethania

Bérenger Saunière

Emma Calve who it is said had an affair with Saunière

Blue Apples that appear reflected into Mary Magdalene
Church on 17th January

The Church Altar of Mary Magdalene Church

Mary Magdalene

Bérenger Saunière

La Tour Magdala

The resting place of Bérenger Saunière and

Marie Denarnaud lies beside him

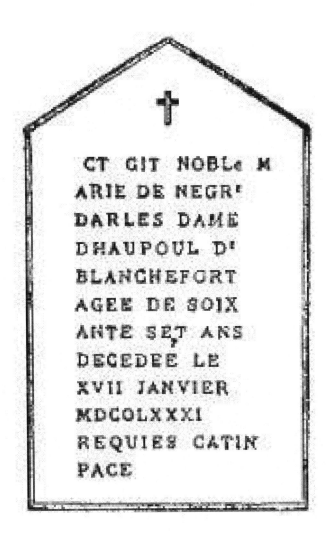

CT GIT NOBLe M
ARIE DE NEGRᵉ
DARLES DAME
DHAUPOUL Dᵉ
BLANCHEFORT
AGEE DE SOIX
ANTE SEP ANS
DECEDEE LE
XVII JANVIER
MDCOLXXXI
REQUIES CATIN
PACE

The writing on the gravestone of

Dame Marie de NEGRE D'ABLES

The first station of the cross

The fourteenth station of the cross

"Did ye never read in the Scriptures, The stone which the builders rejected, the same is become the head of the corner: this is the Lord's doing, and it is marvelous in our eyes?"

(Matt. 21:42).

Salvator Mundi is a painting by Italian artist Leonardo da Vinci, dated to c. 1500. The painting shows Jesus in Renaissance dress, making the sign of the cross with his right hand.

MARY MAGDALENE by Guido Reni (1575-1642)

The Gospel of Mary Magdalene

Chapter 4

(Pages 1 to 6 of the manuscript, containing chapters 1 - 3, are lost. The extant text starts on page 7...)

. . . Will matter then be destroyed or not?

22) The Savior said, All nature, all formations, all creatures exist in and with one another, and they will be resolved again into their own roots.

23) For the nature of matter is resolved into the roots of its own nature alone.

24) He who has ears to hear, let him hear.

25) Peter said to him, Since you have explained everything to us, tell us this also: What is the sin of the world?

26) The Savior said There is no sin, but it is you who make sin when you do the things that are like the nature of adultery, which is called sin.

27) That is why the Good came into your midst, to the essence of every nature in order to restore it to its root.

28) Then He continued and said, That is why you become sick and die, for you are deprived of the one who can heal you.

29) He who has a mind to understand, let him understand.

30) Matter gave birth to a passion that has no equal, which proceeded from something contrary to nature. Then there arises a disturbance in its whole body.

31) That is why I said to you, Be of good courage, and if you are discouraged be encouraged in the presence of the different forms of nature.

32) He who has ears to hear, let him hear.

33) When the Blessed One had said this, He greeted them all,saying, Peace be with you. Receive my peace unto yourselves.

34) Beware that no one lead you astray saying Lo here or lo there! For the Son of Man is within you.

35) Follow after Him!

36) Those who seek Him will find Him.

37) Go then and preach the gospel of the Kingdom.

38) Do not lay down any rules beyond what I appointed you, and do not give a law like the lawgiver lest you be constrained by it.

39) When He said this He departed.

Chapter 5

1) But they were grieved. They wept greatly, saying, How shall we go to the Gentiles and preach the gospel of the Kingdom of the Son of Man? If they did not spare Him, how will they spare us?

2) Then Mary stood up, greeted them all, and said to her brethren, Do not weep and do not grieve nor be irresolute, for His grace will be entirely with you and will protect you.

3) But rather, let us praise His greatness, for He has prepared us and made us into Men.

4) When Mary said this, she turned their hearts to the Good, and they began to discuss the words of the Savior.

5) Peter said to Mary, Sister we know that the Savior loved you more than the rest of woman.

6) Tell us the words of the Savior which you remember which you know, but we do not, nor have we heard them.

7) Mary answered and said, What is hidden from you I will proclaim to you.

8) And she began to speak to them these words: I, she said, I saw the Lord in a vision and I said to Him, Lord I saw you today in a vision. He answered and said to me,

9) Blessed are you that you did not waver at the sight of Me.

For where the mind is there is the treasure.

10) I said to Him, Lord, how does he who sees the vision see it, through the soul or through the spirit?

11) The Savior answered and said, He does not see through the soul nor through the spirit, but the mind that is between the two that is what sees the vision and it is [...]

(pages 11 - 14 are missing from the manuscript)

Chapter 8:

. . . it.

10) And desire said, I did not see you descending, but now I see you ascending. Why do you lie since you belong to me?

11) The soul answered and said, I saw you. You did not see me nor recognize me. I served you as a garment and you did not know me.

12) When it said this, it (the soul) went away rejoicing greatly.

13) Again it came to the third power, which is called ignorance.

14) The power questioned the soul, saying, Where are you going? In wickedness are you bound. But you are bound; do not judge!

15) And the soul said, Why do you judge me, although I have not judged?

16) I was bound, though I have not bound.

17) I was not recognized. But I have recognized that the All is being dissolved, both the earthly things and the heavenly.

18) When the soul had overcome the third power, it went upwards and saw the fourth power, which took seven forms.

19) The first form is darkness, the second desire, the third ignorance, the fourth is the excitement of death, the fifth is the kingdom of the flesh, the sixth is the foolish wisdom of flesh, the seventh is the wrathful wisdom. These are the seven powers of wrath.

20) They asked the soul, Whence do you come slayer of men, or where are you going, conqueror of space?

21) The soul answered and said, What binds me has been slain, and what turns me about has been overcome,

22) and my desire has been ended, and ignorance has died.

23) In a aeon I was released from a world, and in a Type from a type, and from the fetter of oblivion which is transient.

24) From this time on will I attain to the rest of the time, of the season, of the aeon, in silence.

Chapter 9

1) When Mary had said this, she fell silent, since it was to this point that the Savior had spoken with her.

2) But Andrew answered and said to the brethren, Say what you wish to say about what she has said. I at least do not believe that the Savior said this. For certainly these teachings are strange ideas.

3) Peter answered and spoke concerning these same things.

4) He questioned them about the Savior: Did He really speak privately with a woman and not openly to us? Are we to turn about and all listen to her? Did He prefer her to us?

5) Then Mary wept and said to Peter, My brother Peter, what do you think? Do you think that I have thought this up myself in my heart, or that I am lying about the Savior?

6) Levi answered and said to Peter, Peter you have always been hot tempered.

7) Now I see you contending against the woman like the adversaries.

8) But if the Savior made her worthy, who are you indeed to reject her? Surely the Savior knows her very well.

9) That is why He loved her more than us. Rather let us be ashamed and put on the perfect Man, and separate as He commanded us and preach the gospel, not laying down any other rule or other law beyond what the Savior said.

10) And when they heard this they began to go forth to proclaim and to preach.

THE END

Made in the USA
Columbia, SC
20 August 2021